From Snow and Rock,
from Chaos

Also by Hayden Carruth

From Snow and Rock, from Chaos

Poems 1965-1972

HAYDEN CARRUTH

A NEW DIRECTIONS BOOK

NOTE: Grateful acknowledgment is extended to the Guggenheim
Foundation and the National Endowment for the Arts for fellowships
granted during the time when these poems were written, and to the
following publications, in which some of the poems first appeared:
*Antaeus, Approach, Colloquy, Field, The Goddard Journal, Kayak,
Kenyon Review, The Lampeter Muse, The Nation, New American
Review, The New York Times, Partisan Review, Poetry Northwest,
Quarterly Review of Literature, The Record, Sumac, Tamarack
Review,* and *Virginia Quarterly Review.* "Storm at White Sands, N.M."
was first published in *Esquire.* "Tabula Rasa," "For RM, 26
December," "The Wife," "I Know, I Remember, But How Can I
Help You," "The End Again," "This Decoration," "Too Tenuous," and
"Rimrock, Where It Is" were originally published in *The Hudson
Review.* "The Cows at Night," "Homecoming," and "Sonnet" first
appeared in *Poetry.*

Manufactured in the United States of America

First published clothbound (ISBN: 0–8112–0468–5) and as
New Directions Paperbook 349 (ISBN: 0–8112–0469–3) in 1973.

Published simultaneously in Canada by McClelland & Stewart Ltd.

New Directions Books are published for James Laughlin
by New Directions Publishing Corporation,
333 Sixth Avenue, New York 10014

From Snow and Rock,
from Chaos

Dedication in These Days

What words can make
seems next to nothing now
a tune a measure

Yet
I have seen you with
your eyes wet
with pleasure for their sake

For this then
these few
for now for you
again

I Could Take

I could take
two leaves
   and give you one.
Would that not be
a kind of perfection?

But I prefer
one leaf
   torn to give you half
     showing

(after these years, simply)
love's complexity in an act,
   the tearing and
     the unique edges—

one leaf (one word) from the two
imperfections that match.

Reverting Still Again

Reverting still again to the hatch from a
safe distance maybe it was like this
an engine idling with internal fire
the bones of the mastodon burning in the
red light of its lost imagined heart
rigidity and chaos statehood and anarchy
four meals a day served with a bell
a sweet sauce to cover roast paranoia
tick tock the clock two feet in a sock
and virginia creeper flaming in october

trying to consume the square brick walls
where red squirrels are fighting like savages
screaming tooth and claw and none is hurt
a system of dikes walls dividing subduing
the sea that nevertheless still rages
like panthers back and forth in the cells
or a harmonica held up to the wind a line
of uniform holes and each one wailing
differently or think of time's favorite
chimp at the typewriter that was where
he lived where he lived where he lived—

Fear and Anger in the Mindless Universe

Evan just had the white birch lined up
   like always

diagonally on the meadow
   at the top of the rise

going to cambridge junction
   the lone birch that made him think

he said
        of his naked daughter

when the stranger from downcountry
        middlebury way

hit the ice patch
        and skidded.

Evan cramped hard left and down
        into the snowbank and sat there

while the snowfields all around turned black-blank
        like a lightbulb burning out

and then turned white again.
        Slowly

(slowly the meteor descending
        bloodspotted feather swimming down the air)

Evan begun to curse
        he said

like an oxhandler with a firstyoked team.
        It worked too

for the stranger
        bled to death in ten minutes

though the ice patch weren't his fault
        and Evan begun to feel better—

he even begun to laugh.
        That was last tuesday week in the forenoon

but now
        he tells it without smiling

quicklike
        looking out the corner of his eye.

For RM, 26 December

> *To be loved means to be consumed. To love*
> *is to give light with inexhaustible oil.*
> —Rilke

Now you are the word *lamp*. Burn
here in the room that has been torn,

tattered & torn, tattered & torn . . .
Often on recent nights the room

grows soft around us, a nimbus, weird
and reassuring, because I say this word,

love loving beyond love. Who understands?
An offering, hilarious, quick, absurd—

do you, dear girl? Inexhaustibly you consume
my uncreation. I am pure, I have become

the word for you. I write
(in the gray end of every night)

myself, who holds in translucent hands
everyone's lost light.

French Hill

Tell, acquaint me
why they care,
men, if they lie

here or there
in finality?
Tell how come

they are so hot
to put the cold bones
they will have got

in this or another
remembered spot?
And if nearby or far

stone stand or
urn repose, tell
how they'll know it—

will they not
have gone all beyond
what knows and what's known,

meadow or grove or any
glory of mount
or glimmering plot?

For inside the skull
if it be winter
what is memory

but the mere ice that will,
before the ash leaves grow,
thaw and rot?

Here's ash in a knot
of smoky wild rose
above the valley

over the river—
is it a green tree
on midsummer day?

Tomorrow it will not
be a smoking ruin
—imagination is done!—

nothing, nothing
it will be
no thing.

Tell, acquaint me
half-dead mind
why

after all the tear-
drenched years
you'd still

when ice
frizzles your jelly
lie

high above valley
and over river
with the ruined ash

the burnt rose
the rain and the winter
and tell me why

it is any use or good
if a stone certify
the name of nothing

up here above
that house known
for love?

If It Were Not for You

Liebe, meine liebe, I had not hoped
to be so poor

      The night winds reach
like the blind breath of the world
in a rhythm without mind, gusting and beating
as if to destroy us, battering our poverty
and all the land's flat and cold and dark
under iron snow

        the dog leaps in the wind
barking, maddened with winter, and his voice
claps again and again down the valley
like tatters of revolutionary pennants

                              birches
cry and hemlocks by the brook
stand hunched and downcast with their hands
in their pockets

Liebe, the world is wild
and without intention

                    how far
this might be from the night of christmas
if it were not for you.

Down the reaching wind
shrieks of starlight bear broken messages
among mountains where shadows plunge
                                        yet our brightness
is unwavering
              Kennst du das land
wo die zitronen blühn, im dunkeln laub
die goldorangen . . .   liebe
art thou singing

It is a question partly
of the tree with our stars and partly
of your radiance brought from the land
where legends flower to this land
but more than these our bright poverty
is a house in the wind and a light
on the mountain

Liebe, our light rekindled
in this remoteness from the other land,
in this dark of the blue mountain where only
the winds gather
     is what we are for the time that we are
     what we know for the time that we know

How gravely and sweetly the poor touch in the dark.

Speaking for Them

August. Hear
the cicadas
splitting their skins.

The bleeding cow
has rubbed her neck on barbed
wire against the flies,

which return, crawling
in her eyes. She looks up,
a sorrow, raising her great
head in slowness, brown eyes rising
like pools in the earth.

Then the elms. There marching
down the knoll by the fence slowly,
a dead march. Shall we have

Memorial Day for the elms,
those veterans? Here are the oldest,
stricken and proud, lifting

poor broken arms in sleeves
of ragged bark.

Blackeyed susans bow their heads,
crazy swallows
turn somersaults in the air.

To Artemis

The fog is departing, let it go. Odor
of the south, carrying what seems your last
intercession,   your final statement—
flakes of light whirling away, a shower—
    moonflakes, sparks
    scurrying through dark trees.

        And the solid cold air
of the Arctic is sliding around us.

Higher now—bright—you assume your
   mystery, a kind of indwelling
   light that looks sourceless
though it is not. Like alloy, bronze, pewter,
so changed, autonomous, remade: the source
becomes unimportant.

   Snow-lined, the branches of trees
vanish, leaving these jagged streaks,
calligraphic light.   The forest
   startles us.

         Tonight there is
no intercession, no power, but only
mystery. We call you queen but that
does not say what you are.   We try
to be like you; help us if you are able.
Whatever we are, these reflections, let us
change them now, let us be silent, cold,
let us be autonomous, bright,

   in this place so remote and altered.

Tabula Rasa

There, an evening star, there again. Above
The torn lovelace of snow, in the far sky
That glows with an afterlight, fading,

The evening star piercing a black tangle
Of trees on the ridge. Shall it be our kiss?
Can we call its sudden singleness,

Its unannounced simplicity, its rage
In the abhorrent distances, its small viridine,
Ours, always ours? Or shall we say

This wintry eloquence is mere affect
Of tattered snow, of tangling black limbs?
Everything reproaches me, everything,

Because we do not stand by Leman's water,
By the onyx columns, entablatures, all
The entablatures, watching the cygnets fade

With Sapphic pathos into a silver night.
Listen, the oboe and the little drum
Make Lulliana where the old whores walk . . .

Do men and women meet and love forthwith?
Or do they think about it? Or do they
In a masque play fated figures *en tragique*?

Perhaps they are those who only stand
In tattered snow and dream of fated things.
The limbs have snatched the star, have eaten it.

Another night, we've lost another day. Nothing
Spoke to us, certainly nothing spoke for us—
The slate is clean. Here therefore is my kiss.

Concerning Necessity

It's quite true we live
in a kind of rural twilight
most of the time giving
our love to the hard dirt
the water and the weeds
and the difficult woods

ho we say drive the wedge
heave the axe run the hand shovel
dig the potato patch
dig ashes dig gravel
tickle the dyspeptic chain saw
make him snarl once more

while the henhouse needs cleaning
the fruitless corn to be cut
and the house is falling to pieces

the car coming apart
the boy sitting and complaining
about something everything anything

this was the world foreknown
though I had thought somehow
probably in the delusion
of that idiot thoreau
that necessity could be saved
by the facts we actually have

like our extreme white birch
clasped in the hemlock's arms
or our baybreasted nuthatch
or our mountain and our stars
and really these things do serve
a little though not enough

what saves the undoubted collapse
of the driven day and the year
is my coming all at once
when she is done in or footsore
or down asleep in the field
or telling a song to a child

coming and seeing her move
in some particular way
that makes me to fall in love
all over with human beauty
the beauty I can't believe
right here where I live.

The Wife

Engrossed hands always
doing something.

Burden and
refrain: blackbirds,

import of flight and rest,
gleam and shadow in the sun tree

scattering to a page.
You are a page of sun.

You are a parchment
of old staves and alien dark diamonds

always new in the playing.
Over sun meadow moving,

stopping, returning
among yellow susans;

or your sun wind dress
flickering at night in the largo

of stove-light.
The fire dies,

you sleep, quiet horn
resonant of sun.

The Ravine

Stones, brown tufted grass, but no water,
it is dry to the bottom. A seedy eye
of orange hawkweed blinks in sunlight
stupidly, a mink bumbles away,
a ringnecked snake among stones lifts its head
like a spark, a dead young woodcock—
long dead, the mink will not touch it—
sprawls in the hatchment of its soft plumage
and clutches emptiness with drawn talons.
This is the ravine today. But in spring it
cascaded, in winter it filled with snow
until it lay hidden completely. In time,
geologic time, it will melt away
or deepen beyond recognition, a huge
gorge. These are what I remember and foresee.
These are what I see here every day,
not things but relationships of things,
quick changes and slow. These are my sorrow,
for unlike my bright admonitory friends
I see relationships, I do not see things.
These, such as they are, every day, every
unique day, the first in time and the last,
are my thoughts, the sequences of my mind.
I wonder what they mean. Every day,
day after day, I wonder what they mean.

Sonnet

Cry, crow,
caw and caw, clawing
on black wings over hot black pines. What's
one more voice?

This morning the spring gave out,
no water in pipe. Hustled to spring, peered
in and saw three salamanders, very pallid;
saw water-level below pipe-end.

No more syphon. What's that? What? *And*
the brook is polluted.
                        Weather going to pot,
each year drier than last, and hotter.

What's the trouble? Long time, 25 years, was I
mad.
            Won through, does anyone know?
            Hey, crow, does anyone know?
I see a chance for peace! What about water?

Homecoming

A road that had wound us 20,000 miles
stops, with a kind of suddenness, at home.

At home and in midsummer. The snow has gone.
July murmurs its dark momentous tones.

The butternut is heavy, heavy the fruit
hung like genitals under the pleated leaves.

Weeds (we call them) marguerite and gromwell
and queen anne's lace, stand tall in the garden,

and one last foxglove stands among them, with one
magenta cloche hung darkly among the lace.

It does not move in the dark unmoving air
yet we almost hear its tolling. Knell on knell

broaden across the haze of afternoon,
conscious indecencies of ceremonious sorrow.

Two deaths, two abstractions. Our absence
was spooked somehow: changes in spite of us

done in the part of the world we had left locked
in safety. One was a favorite pine and the other

was old Steve Washer. The pine stood shining
in snow when we last saw it, but the rust

took it, and now even in death it is beautiful,
a russet tree in the dark woods. Eventually

its use will serve our fire; we cannot mourn it long.
But Mr. Washer's dying was not like this.

It has no beauty, no usefulness, it is
ugly and stupid, nothing but stupid. It hurts us.

Eighty-five years is long enough to live,
people say; and he was vigorous to the end.

And truly he was, as these said things are true
and good and wise, and in no way disguises,

since the very ones who say them shake their heads
over their own indecent and ceremonious words.

Mr. Washer was a free-born man
who in the toil of self-creation probably wished

he wasn't often enough, and so was like us all;
his loss, as ours will be, is irreplaceable.

That is understood. The man is gone. And then . . .
the type is almost gone, the tough hardminded Yankee

who loved John Locke and let John Bunyan go.
Mr. Washer was the only person who ever respected

our privacy, not partly, not indifferently, but absolutely;
yet was eager to share if asked, our labor or luck

as our need demanded. He was a small man, and lean;
weighed 130 in his prime and somewhat less

toward the end, but could heap grain sacks in the loft
faster than the mill boys could heave them up,

and could walk switchback behind his team all day
in the high fields. He was doing it last July.

Mr. Washer is gone, and in any useful sense
his virtues are gone with him. Our absence

has returned to absence. We walk in our high grass,
restless and petulant among weeds and spiderwebs.

The day is quiet, dark, and hot, but it will not rain.
After all the bell in the garden is silent.

Once More

Once more by the brook the alder leaves
turn mauve, bronze, violet, beautiful
after the green of crude summer; galled
black stems, pithy, tangled, twist in the
flesh-colored vines of wild cyclamen.
Mist drifts below the mountaintop
in prismatic tatters. The brook is full,
spilling down heavily, loudly, in silver
spate from the beaver ponds in the high
marshy meadows. The year is sinking:
heavily, loudly, beautifully. Deer move
heavily in the brush like bears, half drunk
on masty acorns and rotten wild apples.
The pileated woodpecker thumps a dead elm
slowly, irregularly, meditatively.
Like a broken telephone a cricket rings
without assertion in dead asters and
goldenrod; asters gone cloudy with seed,
goldenrod burnt and blackened. A gray trout
rests under the lip of glacial stone. One
by one the alder leaves plunge down to earth,
veering, and lie there, glowing, like a shirt
of Nessus. My heart in my ribs does what it
has done occasionally all my life: thumps and
heaves suddenly in irregular rhythm that makes
me gasp. How many times has this season turned

and gone down? How many! I move heavily
into the bracken, and the deer stand still
a moment, uncertain, before they break away,
snorting and bounding heavily before me.

The Cows at Night

The moon was like a full cup tonight,
too heavy, and sank in the mist
soon after dark, leaving for light

faint stars and the silver leaves
of milkweed beside the road,
gleaming before my car.

Yet I like driving at night
in summer and in Vermont:
the brown road through the mist

of mountain-dark, among farms
so quiet, and the roadside willows
opening out where I saw

the cows. Always a shock
to remember them there, those
great breathings close in the dark.

I stopped, taking my flashlight
to the pasture fence. They turned
to me where they lay, sad

and beautiful faces in the dark,
and I counted them—forty
near and far in the pasture,

turning to me, sad and beautiful
like girls very long ago
who were innocent, and sad

because they were innocent,
and beautiful because they were
sad. I switched off my light.

But I did not want to go,
not yet, nor knew what to do
if I should stay, for how

in that great darkness could I explain
anything, anything at all.
I stood by the fence. And then

very gently it began to rain.

The Spanish Civil War

Thirty years ago tonight
   this bitter night
the spanish civil war began
   o my dear

someone
   we see dimly
   having now remembered him
was wound up tight
with a key in his back
   too tight

But notice the moon glowing on snow
on the palegray snow where it creeps
at the edge of the palegreen pasture
   in the season of going under
and the gray moon shining thirty years ago
on the palegray lemon grove where earth
sparkled with mica and a few bees buzzed
in the dark
   a few latewandering bullets

someone very stiffly crawling
shaking his stiffened head
moves like a black toy on the appalling
earth   and someone

moves at the edge of the pasture
coming this way
  to bed

to bed my dear
for the spanish civil war
spread and spread
  always spreading
and the armies gathered
  always gathering
  in every gathering place
and the world creeps
  the whole world always creeping
to the lemon grove
  our neighbors creeping gathering
  vicious and cruel with eyes like mica

My dear this is my song
of a country
  that it was lovely in the dawn
  that it was garlanded an ox for a lady
  that it was a clear call musical in the field
  that it was a wall but not too high to see over
  that it was rebellious as much of the old as the young
  that it was inquisitive
  that it was a welcome
  that it was born in the woman who lives in the stone
  that it was built by the men who could hew and finger

that it   began even so in a space ravaged from
         a noble people and that it proceeded
         in the only course open to such beginning
         a study and cultivation of death and of
         all manner of degradation and that it
         is a brain rotted in cowardice a heart
         squirming and white
that it is venality   avarice   and the selling
   of authority
whereby the hands of cowards are strengthened
   for cowardly ends
while the old rage in dark houses and the young
   parade   shadows in the streets
and the protestation of murder has been made
   a sin

that it is

o my dear
   in this thirtieth
     year of awakening

my song is
   bitter as the night
     and exhausted

What was born then has no ending
   has come nearer and nearer
like the contagion in the forest
   like the disequilibrium of the seas

Remoteness
and death in the lemon grove
　　under the gray moon
have crept homeward
　　turning my tears to stone

Truly my life has been lived in an evil time

Look
the dark man creeping
where snow drives its blunt edge across the pasture
　　in our november
moving stiffly　　　jerking his head
　　like a broken toy
moving with difficulty toward our window
lighted by the palegray moon
　　in this forgotten corner of the land

soon
he will be in your bed
in your warmth and privacy

Perhaps finally he will not know what to do
and then you must decide
　　quickly
　　for you had not thought this would happen
how you will receive the last shred
　　of the love of the world.

Emergency Haying

Coming home with the last load I ride standing
on the wagon tongue, behind the tractor
in hot exhaust, lank with sweat,

my arms strung
awkwardly along the hayrack, cruciform.
Almost 500 bales we've put up

this afternoon, Marshall and I.
And of course I think of another who hung
like this on another cross. My hands are torn

by baling twine, not nails, and my side is pierced
by my ulcer, not a lance. The acid in my throat
is only hayseed. Yet exhaustion and the way

my body hangs from twisted shoulders, suspended
on two points of pain in the rising
monoxide, recall that greater suffering.

Well, I change grip and the image
fades. It's been an unlucky summer. Heavy rains
brought on the grass tremendously, a monster crop,

but wet, always wet. Haying was long delayed.
Now is our last chance to bring in
the winter's feed, and Marshall needs help.

We mow, rake, bale, and draw the bales
to the barn, these late, half-green,
improperly cured bales; some weigh 100 pounds

or more, yet must be lugged by the twine
across the field, tossed on the load, and then
at the barn unloaded on the conveyor

and distributed in the loft. I help—
I, the desk-servant, word-worker—
and hold up my end pretty well too; but God,

the close of day, how I fall down then. My hands
are sore, they flinch when I light my pipe.
I think of those who have done slave labor,

less able and less well prepared than I.
Rose Marie in the rye fields of Saxony,
her father in the camps of Moldavia

and the Crimea, all clerks and housekeepers
herded to the gaunt fields of torture. Hands
too bloodied cannot bear

even the touch of air, even
the touch of love. I have a friend
whose grandmother cut cane with a machete

and cut and cut, until one day
she snicked her hand off and took it
and threw it grandly at the sky. Now

in September our New England mountains
under a clear sky for which we're thankful at last
begin to glow, maples, beeches, birches

in their first color. I look
beyond our famous hayfields to our famous hills,
to the notch where the sunset is beginning,

then in the other direction, eastward,
where a full new-risen moon like a pale
medallion hangs in a lavender cloud

beyond the barn. My eyes
sting with sweat and loveliness. And who
is the Christ now, who

if not I? It must be so. My strength
is legion. And I stand up high
on the wagon tongue in my whole bones to say

woe to you, watch out
you sons of bitches who would drive men and women
to the fields where they can only die.

First Night

Sunset whirling the storm away, the white disk
swept in change of light, like seabirds,
the snow flock, whirling in lavender, down
the valley, slantward, resettling
in the far impasse. A silent star,
another, sudden green in lavender,
lucid made present in limpid; the sky
is a faint dial. Absurd but not laughable,
the moon lurks on the left, hugely yellow
behind firs darkpointing the horizon. And briefly
everything rests.
                    Pine grosbeaks
in thick boughs nearby make evensong,
premonitive and low. *Loo, loo,* unseen. The trees
might be singing.
                    Now therefore this night
falls. An intensification, a shift of the loom.
Swift moonlight brightening, the north moving across
the snowcrust, valley and hill
glazed in change; for this is the first night
of the hundred nights of winter.
                              An elm,
its choric limbs upraised, drips
cold moonfire gleaming without sound, spilling
without flow or movement down
                    the rim of the hill.

The Far-removed Mountain Men

No salt here, old sea father, holy giant.
We season our nauseous venison
with its own blood.

No cape, no black rock
gleaming in spume, no promontory
touching the eternal waters.

No shifting waterlights far out when a storm
breaks into pieces and the mist
scatters like leaves in windy sunlight.

No grace of gull-flight over our mountains,
no spangle of sea wave below,
no song of a long wind in the dunes.

No tides!
—flood, ebb, spring and neap, beating slow heart,
the measure we dream, the measure we almost feel.

How the seine must rock in that dance!
How the molluscs must snuggle
in their concordant drumming blood!

Snow seeps in our cove. Our starving owl
hunts blind by day, battering the pines.
All night the hours squeak across our sky.

At least will you come to us, old one,
in the spring rains, will you walk
in our fog, surgent among moist firs?

Bring us the great spring-tide mounting
and the salts of love-sweat again.

The Insomniac Sleeps Well for Once and

rises at five, just when a late moon
rises, huge, out of the snow cloud

at the end of the garden. You sleep.
Coming so tired and worried to middle age,

you'll sleep ten hours if we let you,
yet now, slept nearly out, you lie as if

this moon had brought from far in the east,
Silesia, your old self who you really are

come to inhabit you, girl of the rye fields
silver and green, and here comes another

moon, another, another, the snow gleams,
and each one brings something

so that your eyes smoothen as if for love,
your fine bone rises under your skin,

you move and smile in the sleeping knowledge
of yourself, as the spirit of this house moves

smiling from mirror to mirror in brightness,
and oh my god look at the sky full of moons,

look at the snow, the girl, look at the day!

This Song

In an afternoon bright with
September, or in an old dissension
bright with fear, I went wandering where
there was purity in white lady's tresses,
hiddenness in peeping bluebottle gentians,

and where many species of goldenrod
and asters made funeral for the lost
summer world, and ferns, taken by frost,
made russet the fields and turned
the waysides yellow and brown.

It struck me that I had wandered all my years
like this, half a century, searching
for the touch that heals, but there is
no touch; searching everywhere for the
look that says *I know*, but there is

no look. This is Vermont, the land
hidden from violent times, far from the center
of life, they say. I walk by the gray brook,
around the knoll, through the pines. Winter
is coming. Searching, searching with my hand,

I feel September's little knives, and with my eyes
I see bright spattered leaves in the matted
grass. I hear this song, if it be a song: these
insistent little bright fearful hesitant
murmurs from high in the old pine trees.

The Birds of Vietnam

(for RM, who knows how to read it)

O bright, O swift and bright,
you flashing among pandanus boughs
    (is that right? pandanus?)

under the great banyan, in and out
the dusky delicate bamboo groves
   (yes? banyan, bamboo?)
low, wide-winged, gliding
over the wetlands and drylands
   (but I have not seen you,
   I do not know your names,
   I do not know
   what I am talking about).

I have seen the road runner and the golden eagle,
the great white heron and the Kirtland's warbler,
   our own endangered species,
and I have worried about them. I have worried
about all our own, seen and unseen,
whooping cranes, condors, white-tailed kites,
and the ivory-bills (certainly gone, all gone!)
the ones we have harried, murdered, driven away
as if we were the Appointed Avengers,
   the Destroyers, the Wrathful Ones
out of our ancestors' offended hearts
at the cruel beginning of the world.
But for what? for whom? why?
   Nobody knows.

And why, in my image of that cindered country,
should I waste my mourning? I will never have
enough. Think of the children there,
insane little crusted kids at the beckoning fire,

think of the older ones, burned, crazy with fear,
sensible beings who can know hell, think
of their minds exploding, their hearts flaming.

I do think. But today,
O mindless, O heartless, in and out
the dusky delicate groves,
your hell becomes mine, simply
and without thought, you maimed, you
poisoned in your nests, starved
in the withered forests.
   O mindless, heartless,
   you never invented hell.
We say flesh turns to dust, though more often
a man-corpse is a bloody pulp,
and a bird-corpse too, yet your feathers
   retain life's color
long afterward, even in the robes
   of barbarous kings,
still golden the trogon feather,
still bright the egret plume, and the crest
of the bower bird will endure forever
almost. You will always remind us of what
   the earth has been.

O bright, swift, gleaming
in dusky groves,
I mourn you.
O mindless, heartless, I can't
help it, I have so loved
   this world.

The Baler

You tourist composed upon that fence
to watch the quaint farmer at his quaint task
come closer, bring your camera here
or fasten your telescopic lens
if you're too indolent; all I ask
is that when you go home you take
a close-up among your color slides
of vacationland, to show we pay the price
for hay, this actual panic: no politic fear
but tumbling wild waves down the windrows, tides
of crickets, grasshoppers, meadow mice,
and half-feathered sparrows, whipped by a bleeding snake.

Storm at White Sands, N. M.

The edge of a dune, wind driven, leans
and spills down the face, again, again.

At the center of the wide brown desert, a white
desert. Wind blurs the light. The storm

is a force too great to be categorized.
Its friction charges the walker with electricity.

He leans to earth to feel the spark click
from his finger. At the summit of the dune

his outline chars, like a film overexposed,
and he stands burning in whiteness, consumed

by sand and storm, by the force without category.
How quick a spark enters the earth and is gone.

I Know, I Remember, But How Can I Help You

The northern lights.   I wouldn't have noticed them
   if the deer hadn't told me
   a doe   her coat of pearls   her glowing hoofs
              proud and inquisitive
              eager for my appraisal
and I went out into the night with electrical steps
   but with my head held also proud
                 to share the animal's fear
                 and see what I had seen before
   a sky flaring and spectral
                 greenish waves and ribbons
and the snow   under strange light   tossing in the pasture
   like a storming ocean caught
                 by a flaring beacon.

The deer stands away from me   not far
                there among bare black apple trees
                a presence I no longer see.
    We are proud to be afraid
                proud to share
the silent magnetic storm that destroys the stars
                and flickers around our heads
    like the saints' cold spiritual agonies
                of old.
I remember   but without the sense   other light-storms
    cold memories discursive and philosophical
                in my mind's burden
    and the deer remembers nothing.
We move our feet   crunching bitter snow   while the storm
    crashes like god-wars down the east
                we shake the sparks from our eyes
    we quiver inside our shocked fur
                we search for each other
    in the apple thicket—
                a glimpse, an acknowledgment
    it is enough and never enough—
we toss our heads   and say good night
    moving away on bitter bitter snow.

The End Again

Moonlight. Metaphorical of
Abstract perfect justice
Whitening white snow, so bright
I read the thermometer: a hair above
Forty below.

Can't talk, arctic air
Scorching my throat. But how
Immense this high tension
System is! With somewhere, we know,
A weak connection fraying
Out there.

It will go. Flare, stink
Of burnt metal, and lights
Out. Absolute zero bursts
In, implosion—a sudden suck.
No cry. Air will freeze
Solid, sound will freeze
Solid, every word
Stuck on a still wave. The tapes
Heaped in a tangle, unplayable.

The moon. Close ornate cornice
In upper foreground to dramatize
Our photo's perspective, a still sweep

To absolute everywhere. Thinking: tonight
Or soon. Everything's trite or classical
And I can't draw the line. Stiff,
Almost solid, staring with frozen eyes.

This Decoration

Blue light, morning
glory color, driven
through green fir boughs,

bright as crow-caw
on the next to last day
of October. You've given

me this decoration
made from dried pasted
flowers inside the cap

of a cottage cheese
carton. Beautiful
flowers, unrecognizable

flowers, at which I stare
with a blue-green feeling,
delighted and ignorant,

until you tell me you
made them up. One
is scales from a pine cone

flattened, with a tuft
of silverrod seedfluff
in the center. Another

from a dried panicle
of millet with petals
of mapleseed. Now

I see burrs, bark, a
snip of duck feather. How
exquisite, flowers

of imagination from this
real world, made and given
for lovingkindness. I

go out, wordless, walking
the stubble rows; and here,
high, comes this black

crow, above the furrows
high and straight, flapping,
as if from a great

distance, from eternity.
Caw caw, loudly. And back
from beyond the firs comes

the answer, *caw*, way off, far
although near too, and wordless,
as real things always are.

Too Tenuous

Thirty yards apart, they face
not each other
but both in the same direction,
and yet could not be more together,
these sandhill cranes near Ruby Lake, Nevada,
two russet paleographic curves, slender
Chinese brushstrokes among tan reeds—
the composed and oriental splendor
of this world. Bo, my son,
you grow as this grows rarer.
We know what the cranes are facing. Already
I am a collector
of such precious fragments and you will become
perhaps a connoisseur, driven in love and wonder
to pedantry. Turn away, dear Bo.
Love will not keep in such a dwindled order
too tenuous to know.

Rimrock, Where It Is

Ruined, time ruined, all these once good things.
The structure of many rooms built in the sun,

a refuge from sun; but its parts have gone
wandering, there down the hillside in flowers.

A few doorways remain, arched gently, open
to a white-hot sky, but through them the spirits

long since ceased to pass. Ladders mount the walls
rung by rung to nowhere. The city of desolation,

creviced for the scorpion, is pierced everywhere
by sun, whose mindless immitigable command

beats down with the same force as when its liege folk
listened: generate, generate. Only scorpions hear,

the female eating the male's head while they couple.
Nearby in a refuge of poured concrete and glass

a small woman, small as a girl, black with time,
lies and lies, always raising her head, her charred face,

always raising her knees in a mock of childbirth,
always opening her mouth that is gagged with dust,

always screaming. It reverberates, wave on wave,
the desert's pulse. And the blind albino

fish, relic of a once vast species, that swims
in the lake at the bottom of the deepest cave

in Arizona, in darkness or in glittering rays
of flashlights, goes round and round and round.

Almost April

North winter
month after month.

From early November until now,
almost April,
snow has fallen and fallen,
drifting upon us
in seethe and murmur.

Month after month
air hobbled with snowflakes.

Hour after hour, all hours
of snow searching, hopeless,
aimless in dark hemlock
or light intricate birch.

I have seen snowflakes
all winter
like blurred stars in the air,
queer tumultuous lights
as if in a mist,
soft bodies
like dead moths falling
from the crowns of poisoned trees.

Stars falling, stars
in multitude, the universe
drifting down—
lights without sound or almost
without sound.

And no end to it.

Walking, lost in stardrift,
only the ghost of the dog to lead me,
alone in whiteness, lost
in a cold void, O Eckhart!
knowledge of this zero moving
across, this flaking, across
nothing, flake among flakes, flung
to nowhere by the breath blown through me,
cold acetylene of the stars!

I can't take it. That once was not
forever. I am still warm inside.

Even there, lost in farthest reality
when I was blest, the sound
of the shot man came.
I press my hands to my lips
to feel my blood and bone.
I don't know what I want, clarity
of light beyond meaning or my howl
pitched with the minstrels who are on the run.
But when a hint of woodsmoke
laces the wind
I smile without thinking.

How wind veers or snow
fills my tracks, no matter.
Directions remain—toward, from,
commitment, refusal. Now
in the abandoned hotel on the mountain
broken glass squeals under the boot
like dead violins, snow
drifts in the corridor like old
conversation. Somewhere a door is always
closing, clapped by the wind, though often
in refusal I go myself
to shut them
softly, with strange reluctance.

Weary, God!
of starfall and snowfall,
weary of north winter, and weary
of myself like this, so cold and thoughtful.

Song

Summer burns on the edges of day
   and nothing changes.
The sea like an old thin opal
   clasped by a thin golden shore
turns past the broken stones of a temple
   on which the butterflies
perch and turn like slowly branching flame.
   A cankerworm spins in the quince tree.

Nothing changes. The woman stares
   outward, holding
one hand to her hair as always,
   her pale eyes
burning. The man searches his pockets
   or tosses his head
like a kite launched in the fiery wind.
   A cankerworm spins in the quince tree.

No word has been spoken. Her eyes are
   the same pale stars
as ever, and she will open to him
   with almost the same smile.
But the day burns as if a thread of fire
   in summer's tapestry
had severed the unicorn from the virgin.
   A cankerworm spins in the quince tree.

Nothing changes. The butterflies
   flare and subside,
the sea rubs sparks from the shore,
   the woman stares
at the gulls far on the fiery wind
   drifting over and out,
the man rubs flame from a match.
   A cankerworm spins in the quince tree.

O masters of revolution, don't you see
   what is the way of change?
Take this man to your cause quickly
   for he is desperate,
and listen to the names he is muttering
   against reality.
He changes the world, the world is changed.
   A cankerworm spins in the quince tree.

Twilight Comes

(after Wang Wei)

Twilight comes to the little farm
At winter's end. The snowbanks
High as the eaves, which melted
And became pitted during the day,

Are freezing again, and crunch
Under the dog's foot. The mountains
From their place behind our shoulders
Lean close a moment, as if for a
Final inspection, but with kindness,
A benediction as the darkness
Falls. It is my fiftieth year. Stars
Come out, one by one with a softer
Brightness, like the first flowers
Of spring. I hear the brook stirring,
Trying its music beneath the ice.
I hear—almost, I am not certain—
Remote tinklings; perhaps sheepbells
On the green side of a juniper hill
Or wineglasses on a summer night.
But no. My wife is at her work,
There behind yellow windows. Supper
Will be soon. I crunch the icy snow
And tilt my head to study the last
Silvery light of the western sky
In the pine boughs. I smile. Then
I smile again, just because I can.
I am not an old man. Not yet.

Abandoned Ranch, Big Bend

Three people come where no people belong any more.
They are a woman who would be young
And good-looking if these now seemed
Real qualities, a child with yellow hair, a man
Hardened in desperate humanity. But here are only
Dry cistern, adobe flaking, a lizard. And now this
Disagreeable feeling that they were summoned. Sun
On the corrugated roof is a horse treading,
A horse with wide wings and heavy hoofs. The lizard
Is splayed head down on the wall, pulsing. They do not
Bother to lift their binoculars to the shimmering distance.
From this dead center the desert spirals away,
Traveling outward and inward, pulsing. Summoned
From half across the world, from snow and rock,
From chaos, they arrived a moment ago, they thought,
In perfect fortuity. There is a presence emerging here in
Sun dance and clicking metal, where the lizard blinks
With eyes whetted for extinction; then swirling
Outward again, outward and upward through the sky's
White-hot funnel. Again and again among the dry
Wailing voices of displaced Yankee ghosts
This ranch is abandoned to terror and the sublime.
The man turns to the woman and child. He has never
Said what he meant. They give him
The steady cool mercy of their unreproachful eyes.

Moon

From Clay Hill, high,
next to the old pitched cultivation
of the settlers' graveyard, I watch you,
eastward of the mountain there
rising, your glowing fervent bronze, so full
though with one edge blurred
as if in sympathy with the settlers lying
half in the blurred
receding shadow of April's snow.
I watch you, alone and lonely,
both of us lonely, full of this late
fire. Then I descend once more
to the cove, to deepening snow and the house
that stands by the loud brook in freshet
under the hemlock bank, finding
my loves there, companionate and always
careful of me. And you
are hidden by banked black boughs,
as I am hidden by love.

                    Hours later
when the night has gone to frost
again, a reversion to winter,
I walk out onto the crusted snow
and there you are, high
in the winter sky again, so clear,

like a free flake in the stream
of stars. I have found you.
I lean to you in the depths
of cold and darkness, you always there
and yet often hidden, as I too
am where I am always, hidden.

Index of Titles and First Lines